Original title:
Icicle Dreams

Author: Mariana Leclair
ISBN HARDBACK: 978-9916-94-550-6
ISBN PAPERBACK: 978-9916-94-551-3

Sojourn in Frostfire

Toothbrush frozen, can't quite brush,
Mouth agape in icy hush.
I slip on frost like a dance floor,
Who knew winter had such a score?

Snowman wears my scarf with flair,
His frosty grin beyond compare.
I told him jokes, he laughed so bright,
Yet he melted by midnight's light.

Glistening Edges of the Past

Mom found my old mittens, quite a plight,
Wondering if they were ever white.
Covered in patches, oh so grand,
An artwork made by a toddler's hand.

Snowball fights went wildly wrong,
Hit the cat; now she sings a song.
She plots revenge, I laugh and run,
Meowed a winter tune, just for fun.

Reflections Beneath the Ice

My breath a cloud, a winter show,
But my nose keeps leading the flow.
I slipped on ice, a graceful glide,
Landed right where my dog resides.

He looks at me with judging eyes,
As if to say, 'What a surprise!'
I grin and toss him frozen treat,
He snorts in laughter, isn't life sweet?

Ethereal Chimes of Winter

Bells that hang from frosty eaves,
But what if they hold tiny thieves?
Squirrels plotting as they leap,
Dreaming of acorns, oh what a creep!

With every slide, I take a chance,
Outsmarted once, now it’s my dance.
I twirl and twizzle, give it some flair,
Winter's surprise—a snowman with hair!

Melodies of the Winter Veil

Frosty tunes on every tree,
A choir of snowflakes singing glee.
With coats so puffy, we waddle on,
Silly slips, and giggles spawn.

Hot cocoa spills, marshmallows fly,
We dance around, but oh my, oh my!
Snowballs launched, a frosty brawl,
Laughter rings, the winter's call.

A Tapestry of Frozen Whimsy

Snowmen grinning with carrot noses,
Wearing boots like winter posers.
Sledding down with wild delight,
We crash at last, what a sight!

Shovels swing like musical sticks,
Heroes of snow, we play our tricks.
Mittens mismatched, silly hats,
Chasing tails of fluffing cats.

Caught in the Grasp of Winter

Bundled tight, can't move my feet,
A dance becomes a wobbly feat.
But then I trip, and oh I roll,
Down the slope, a frozen stroll!

Eager ghosts in snowflakes twirl,
Invisible friends in a frosty whirl.
As snowflakes land on my nose with care,
I giggle out loud, warmth in the air.

Whispers of Enchanted Snowflakes

Snowflakes whisper secrets shared,
Cotton candy visions, all prepared.
A frosty wind, it gives a tease,
While snowflakes prance like silly bees.

Laughing children on the street,
Chasing joy, our hearts skip a beat.
Let's build a fort, with walls of snow,
In this chilly world, let fun overflow!

Glistening Memories of Winter

In my yard, the snowflakes swoop,
Like kittens playing in a loop.
My nose turns red, my cheeks are bright,
Chasing snowmen—a silly sight!

Glistening roofs like sugar peaks,
I trip on ice, then lose my sneaks.
With laughter echoing through the air,
I dance and slip without a care.

Nightfall's Frostbite Kiss

The moon peeks out, a frosty tease,
I make a wish on winter's freeze.
A snowball lands right on my hat,
I turn around; it's just my cat!

She's plotting schemes with snowy paws,
While I am tangled in my flaws.
The stars wink down, a silent cheer,
As I let out a goofy cheer.

Frozen Echoes of Innocence

In the playground, laughter flies,
Snowmen wear my sister’s eyes.
Winter coats puff out like clouds,
We strut around, feeling so proud.

But slips and falls bring blushing glee,
As snowflakes tickle our bumblebee.
We roll and tumble, an icy dance,
Life's frosty moments—let's take a chance!

The Weight of Silent Frost

The world is blanketed in white,
Snowflakes whisper, soft and light.
My boots are heavy, my smile wide,
As I pretend to glide and slide.

Chasing shadows through the trees,
Each crunch beneath brings giggling pleas.
Winter wraps us in its spell,
Oh, frozen shenanigans, do tell!

Flickering Hopes Beneath the Snow

In winter's chill, the penguins dance,
They wobble and slip, a comical prance.
Snowflakes tickle their feathered cheeks,
In fluffy coats, they twirl unique peaks.

Snowmen grin with carrot noses,
Complimented by the smirk of roses.
Frosty, they giggle, their hats askew,
While children throw snowballs, a playful brew.

Frigid Whispers

The trees wear coats, all lacy white,
They shiver and quiver, a funny sight.
Branches whisper jokes to the frosty air,
While squirrels bounce ‘round without a care.

A snowball fights in the park take flight,
Kids giggling madly, what a delight!
Their laughter echoes in the frosty scene,
As snowflakes wear crowns of purest sheen.

A Waltz with Winter's Edge

The skaters twirl on a frozen lake,
As ducks quack humor, for goodness' sake.
They slip and slide, then tumble down,
Each face shows laughs, none hold a frown.

Winter jackets puff like marshmallows sweet,
With scarves that whip in a chilly beat.
Snowflakes giggle as they land on noses,
As frosty fingers brush off frozen roses.

Frost-dusted Mirages

The sun peeks out in a shy ballet,
Frosty friends play hide and seek each day.
With hot cocoa, they sip, then spill,
Their laughter bubbles like a winter thrill.

A snow globe tumbles, it’s all out of whack,
Tiny scenes whirling like a wild track.
Each shake brings giggles, a shimmering jest,
In a world of cold, humor’s the best.

Songs of the Winter Whisper

Snowflakes dance like they're on a spree,
Not one of them plans to stay with me.
They twirl around in a chilly ballet,
Then melt like my hopes, what a sad display.

Each breath I take is a frosty puff,
My nose is red; are we having enough?
The dog looks puzzled, caught in a freeze,
He thinks the snow is the world's largest cheese.

Sledding down hills with a squeaky shout,
I bounce on a bump and slip right out.
The snowman I built? He's a lumpy mess,
With a carrot nose that's now in distress.

Winter whispers secrets, all made of chill,
Tickling my toes, giving me a thrill.
But as I trip on a patch of the white,
I laugh at myself, what a goofy sight!

Shivering Colors in the Snow

Purple mittens clash with my bright red coat,
Each step I take makes a squishy note.
Snowballs are flying, a playful attack,
But I'm the one dodging, I can't fight back!

The birds in the trees can barely take flight,
In search of some seeds, they'll dine in delight.
Chirps turn to chattering, are they having fun?
They seem more confused than anyone!

Slip on a patch, and whoa, there I go,
Skating on ice like a clown in a show.
At least the kids laugh with every fall,
My slip-and-slide dance is a hit at the mall!

A snow fort is built, oh what a grand sight,
With gummy bear guards, all ready to bite.
My friends and I plot, what a scheme we've spun,
Winter may be cold, but it's full of fun!

Whispered Promises of Winter

In the chill, snowmen grin wide,
Their carrot noses, a funny pride.
Shovels dance with a frosty beat,
Snowflakes twirl with whimsical feet.

Sleds race down, laughter in the air,
Hot cocoa spills, no one seems to care.
Snowball fights bring giggles and glee,
As winter whispers, come play with me!

The Silent Melting

From rooftops drip a silent song,
As snowmen droop, it won’t be long.
One eye asks where the summer's play,
While puddles grumble, 'We're here to stay!'

The sun warms up with a cheeky grin,
Wishing for sunscreen, not a wintry pin.
A snowflake's fate is a wicked tease,
Turning to water with relative ease.

Tapestry of Winter Shards

Frosty patterns on window panes,
Look like doodles from playful brains.
Crisp air laughs with each chilly breath,
While squirrels plot their frosty theft.

Each shard of ice, a crystal laugh,
Reflecting joy in nature's craft.
Glistening roads, a slippery trail,
As winter's humor begins to wail.

Glinting Dreams in the Frost

Winter plays tricks with a sly little wink,
Pretending to freeze while we all rethink.
Shiny like gems, the snowflakes quirk,
As kids tumble down with a playful jerk.

Mittens lost in the frosty bite,
Hands frozen, but spirits alight.
From hot choco mugs, marshmallows plop,
Dancing on whipped cream, they never stop!

Mirrored in Solstice's Gaze

In winter's chill, my breath takes flight,
I make a mustache, oh what a sight!
The mirror laughs, reflecting me,
A frosty clown, oh can't you see?

The sunlight sparkles, a dance of cheer,
Snowflakes giggle, my nose draws near.
With every sip of hot cocoa bliss,
I can’t help but laugh at winter's kiss.

A Dance on the Edge of Cold

I glide on ice, like a chicken in heels,
Flapping my arms, oh how it feels!
I slip and slide, a wobbly show,
A ballet of laughter, as I go low.

My friends cheer on, they can’t contain,
Rolling in snow, they go insane.
We twirl and tumble, no grace in sight,
A comedy sketch in the cold moonlight.

Starlit Frost Crystals

Under the stars, with ice on my nose,
I'm building snowmen, in mismatched clothes!
They wink and giggle, my frosty crew,
Fashion disasters, but I love them too.

One has a carrot, another a hat,
Oh look, that one seems to be a cat!
In this frozen world, oh what a scene,
Laughter dances, fresh and keen.

Shards of Solitude

In a frozen void where silence reigns,
I talk to snowflakes, like they're my chains.
They chuckle softly, float down with ease,
While I try to catch them, the effort's a tease.

A little snowman fills the void with glee,
He’s nodding wisely, or is it just me?
With each frosty breath, I giggle aloud,
In this icy silence, I’m joyfully proud.

Echoes from the Frozen Vale

In a land where snowmen dance,
A penguin slips, takes a chance.
He twirls around with silly glee,
Chasing snowflakes—set them free!

Chill winds whisper secrets bold,
A carrot nose turns to solid gold.
Snowballs fly with laughter loud,
As snowflakes gather like a crowd.

Frosty hats and mittens clash,
In the snow, they make a splash.
Snow angels giggle, create a scene,
In frozen dreams, they're carefree and keen.

Giggles blanket the frozen ground,
As playful pups leap all around.
The winter sun gives a cheeky grin,
In this chilly realm, let fun begin!

Winter's Glimmering Secrets

A snowman blinks with buttons bright,
He sings off-key, a silly sight.
His carrot top is tipped just so,
Pretending he’s a star of show!

Underneath the frosty trees,
Rabbits hop, making a tease.
Snowballs whirl with cheeky glee,
Nature’s giggles fill the spree.

Icicles dangle like great spears,
Yet they drip and bring us cheers.
Silly hats fall, a funny spree,
While squirrels plan their next big shee.

The frozen pond becomes a stage,
Where critters act their funny page.
All of winter sings in jest,
In this glimmering world, we’re blessed!

Shattered Mirrors of Light

Glassy shards catch winter's ray,
A kaleidoscope of bright ballet.
Snowflakes fall like tiny jesters,
Each one grinning, no time for testers.

Frosted windows tell a tale,
Of snowball fights that never pale.
A burst of laughter, whoosh and roll,
In this glimmer, we're all on a stroll.

The sun plays tag with snowy swirls,
While frosty twirls become frozen pearls.
Dancing shadows, a chilly spark,
Blanket laughter, hear the banter in the park.

Giggling gales blow through the pines,
Where furry faces draw funny lines.
Each sparkling droplet, a merry sight,
Turns winter's chill into pure delight.

Frost-kissed Reveries

In a world where snowflakes reign,
The puppy bumps his little brain.
Chasing tails in endless lines,
He trips and laughs, oh what fun signs!

Frost-kissed dreams dance in the air,
Little children spin without a care.
Snowmen wobble, hats askew,
In this frosty game, there’s always new!

The chilly breeze tickles cheeks,
While whimsical laughter is what it seeks.
Snowball battles, playful and bright,
Turn winter's gloom into pure delight.

As shadows stretch and daylight fades,
Winter whispers through the glades.
In frozen reveries, fun takes flight,
Delighting all in joyful light!

Tapped by Nature's Hand

Frozen droplets hang like jests,
Nature giggles at her best.
Winking at the passing breeze,
They dance upon the winter trees.

A comic show of glistened light,
Chasing shadows, taking flight.
They tease the sun with shimm'ring glee,
Who knew frost could be so free?

Mischief sparkles on each ledge,
As they dangle, form a pledge.
To crack and pop in warmth's embrace,
Fooling all with frosty grace.

In every drip, a secret told,
Of laughter that the cold must hold.
Nature's giggle, crisp and tight,
Leaves us smiling in delight.

Glistening Pathways of Time

Slippery streets with sparkles bright,
Every step a dance of light.
We laugh as we slip and slide,
On this frosty, glimmering ride.

Each pathway sparkles, oh so grand,
Nature's folly at her hand.
We wander forth with silly glee,
As the ice plays tricks on me.

Beneath the clouds, a jester’s stage,
Backflips performed on winter's page.
With every crunch and every fall,
We hear winter's funny call.

Glistening moments, fleeting fast,
Frozen fun that cannot last.
Yet we'll cherish each bright fling,
And let the frozen laughter ring.

Enchanted by the Chill

Frosty whispers in the air,
Kissed by cold could be a dare.
With every shiver, smiles abound,
Nature's quirkiness is profound.

Snowflakes tickle all our noses,
While winter's charm just overposes.
Bundle up in hats and scarves,
As we navigate its little farce.

An ice sculpture that's awry,
Looks like a bird that loves to fly.
Each frozen thing a silly sight,
Gleefully wrapped in winter's light.

Yet laughter warms the chilly thrill,
As we embrace this quirky chill.
In every frostbite prank we see,
Winter's magic sets us free.

The Quiet of Shards

In morning's light, the shards appear,
A jigsaw puzzle, crystal clear.
They shimmer softly, giggles blend,
With sunlight as the perfect friend.

Crunch underfoot, a snap and crack,
Each little shard is coming back.
Nature's puzzle, made for fun,
Creating joy with everyone.

A prism dance in bright display,
With each shard having its own say.
They whisper secrets of the night,
In a language of frosty delight.

So let us play upon this stage,
As laughter wraps around each edge.
The quiet beauty always shares,
A funny tale of winter's cares.

Glacial Mosaics

In winter's chill, we slip and slide,
With frozen paths where we collide.
A snowball flies, it hits the mark,
Who knew the snow could leave a spark?

Our shovels dance like clumsy fools,
As neighbors stare and call us mules.
We build a fort, it's way too small,
But snowball fights can win it all!

A snowman grins with a crooked nose,
His stick arms flail, a sight that glows.
But watch out, he starts to sway,
A gentle breeze can save the day!

So grab your scarf, and join the fun,
In glacial art, you're never done.
With laughter ringing through the air,
These frosty dreams are beyond compare.

Sparkling Veins of Memory

The sun reflects on icy streams,
Creating paths for silly schemes.
A slip, a slide, a soaring leap,
In frosty lands, no time for sleep!

We race our shadows on the ice,
With giggles sweet and bold advice.
Don't eat the snow, it’s yellow, friend,
Unless you wish for a funny end!

We carve our names on snowy sheets,
While penguin dances fill the streets.
Each tumble down brings shouts of glee,
A winter wonderland, oh me!

Sparkling veins twist through the air,
With memories that we can’t compare.
Let’s freeze these moments, keep them tight,
In every laugh, the heart takes flight.

Frosted Lullabies

In blankets thick of snowy white,
We tell tall tales by candlelight.
A fox walks by in playful run,
While snowflakes fall, oh what fun!

The chilly air brings happy shrieks,
As children frolic, laughter peaks.
A balmy breath, a dance of grace,
Where chilly cheeks meet winter's face.

Hot cocoa warms our frozen hands,
With marshmallows forming frosty bands.
In dreams we ride our sleds and fly,
With snowmen waving from nearby.

Frosted lullabies softly hum,
Of candy roads and sugar plums.
Through winter’s night, our hearts will sway,
In cozy warmth, where joy’s at play.

Secrets Weaved in the Cold

The secret paths are wide and bright,
With giggles echoing through the night.
We twist and turn in snowy mazes,
Finding treasure in frozen phases.

A sled careens with joyous glee,
Bumping bumps with agony.
“Ooops!” you cry, as you fly high,
In this winter circus, oh my, oh my!

Mittens lost and scarves entwined,
Fuzzy hats just mismatched, you’ll find.
But in the chaos, hearts will glow,
In laughter shared through winter's flow.

Secrets whispered ‘neath the frost,
No chilly moment is ever lost.
In icy realms where memories unfold,
We spin our tales — no need to be bold!

Beneath the Shimmering Surface

Beneath the frost, a secret lies,
A tiny fish with big surprise.
It wears a hat, quite out of place,
Swimming with style, a dazzling grace.

The snowflakes dance, a goofy crew,
They swirl and twirl in a waltz, it's true.
One dizzy flake trips on a shard,
And lands on a penguin, oh, how bizarre!

A winter sun can't help but laugh,
At the snowmen's battle, a comical gaff.
One's got a carrot, the other a broom,
But they both end up stuck in a room!

In this chill, a merry cheer,
With frosty friends who cannot steer.
They slide on ice, their giggles flare,
Beneath the shimmer, joy fills the air.

Liquid Ice and Midnight's Glow

In the night, a puddle gleams,
Reflecting stars in frozen dreams.
A cat tiptoes, thinks it's wise,
But slips and performs a ballet surprise.

A snowman in shades strikes a pose,
Hoping to catch winter's frivolous flows.
With carrot nose and a scarf askew,
He winks at a bird that squeaks, 'Me too!'

Under moonlight, the world gets punk'd,
Squirrels in parkas, the trees all junked.
They skate in circles, a wobbly fleet,
Chasing each other on little cold feet.

So raise a cup to winter's jest,
In this frosty frame, we're truly blessed.
With laughter echoing, let joy expand,
In liquid ice, we take a stand.

Tinsel Among the Snowflakes

Tinsel drips from trees so tall,
Sprinkling glitter where snowflakes fall.
An ornament rolls, with a clatter and bump,
Rolling down the hill, oh what a lump!

The reindeer prance in clunky shoes,
Mixing up the holiday blues.
They giggle and jingle, then take a spin,
Two tangled up, let the fun begin!

Chasing each other in a flurry of white,
Christmas lights blink in sheer delight.
Sleds fly by, all helter-skelter,
As laughter echoes, hearts begin to melt here.

So grab a hot drink and feel the glow,
Among the flakes, let the good times flow.
Tinsel shines bright on this winter's day,
With joyful hearts, we all play!

Spheres of Chilled Hope

Snowballs form with a frosty cheer,
Launched with laughter, they disappear.
The dog catches one, thinks it's a treat,
Only to find it's a chilly defeat!

A penguin slides on a banana peel,
Wobbling around, what a slippery deal!
He quacks in surprise as he twists and sways,
Fumbling through snow in the silliest ways.

Snowflakes tumble, a whimsical sight,
Tickling your nose in the frosty night.
They chuckle and giggle as they drift down low,
Painting the world with a pure, happy glow.

So toss a snowball and join in the fun,
Let’s make some mischief ’til the day is done.
With spheres of hope, we laugh and we play,
In this wintry realm, we sing and sway!

Ethereal Veil of Winter's Breath

In the chill of frosty air,
A snowman grins, without a care.
He wears a hat that's far too wide,
Yet boasts about his frosty pride.

Beneath the trees, the shadows play,
As snowflakes dance in bright ballet.
The squirrels slide on frozen ground,
While giggles and laughter abound.

Hot cocoa spills with every sip,
Marshmallows float like a snowdrift ship.
A penguin waddles down the lane,
Complaining 'bout the cold and rain.

Magic sparkles, cold and sweet,
As winter hosts a clumsy feat.
We twirl and slip on ice so slick,
And laugh when we fall – what a trick!

Shivering Harmonies

A chorus sings in winter's light,
With shivers dancing left and right.
The frosty notes slip through the air,
As snowball fights bring frantic flair.

The penguins wear their tuxedos proud,
Parading through the icy crowd.
With flippers flapping, they unite,
Intent on causing pure delight.

Each chilly laugh, a playful tease,
As biting winds play with our knees.
Yet in this freeze, we find a way,
To warm our hearts with games we play.

A snowman trips and starts to roll,
His carrot nose forgets its goal.
And as he tumbles, we all cheer,
The winter jest is crystal clear!

Liquid Light and Snow's Embrace

Glittering drops from branches swing,
As sunlight makes the winter sing.
A cup of joy spills down the street,
While snowflakes tickle our cold feet.

A dog in boots runs fast and wide,
With snowy paws, he takes a glide.
He leaps and bounds, a furry clown,
Making us laugh while tumbling down.

The frosty air is light and bright,
As kittens chase the gleams of white.
They pounce on fluff, but then they sneeze,
The world of dreams wrapped up in freeze.

Down winter's path, we skip and hop,
A joyful group, we never stop.
Each chilly breath a burst of cheer,
As winter spreads its magic near!

Dreaming in Frost's Embrace

We wander through this snow-glazed land,
With rosy cheeks and gloves so grand.
The stars above in cold repose,
Watch over all our winter woes.

A snowball flies, a direct hit,
It lands right on my buddy's mitt.
With laughter ringing through the air,
The game goes on without a care.

In cozy huts, we share our snacks,
Hot cookies, treats, all on our backs.
With every bite, a giggle spills,
As winter warms, it brings us thrills.

The icy wind, it plays a tune,
While cute raccoons dance 'neath the moon.
In frosty dreams, we twirl and sway,
And bid the winter chill, “Hooray!”

Unraveling Dreams in the Designed Cold.

A penguin slipped on early morn,
Trying to dance but ended up worn.
He twirled, he swayed, then boom, down he went,
In a frosty puddle, all dignity spent.

Snowflakes giggle from above the tree,
As a rabbit hops, thinking he's free.
He leaped too high, got stuck on a branch,
Hanging upside down, in a wintery stance.

The sun pokes out to warm the snow,
But all it does is make the ice glow.
A snowman sneezes, his carrot flies,
Landing in the soup of the chef’s surprise.

When winter chills our playful hearts,
We laugh at how the cold imparts.
For in the freeze, we find a cheer,
In clumsy slips, and smiles so sheer.

Frosted Whispers

Frosty whispers dance in the breeze,
Telling tales with giggles and tease.
A polar bear lets out a yawn,
Then waves goodbye to a sleepy dawn.

Squirrels chatter with cheeks so round,
Hiding acorns that can’t be found.
One lost his stash among the snow,
Now the birds grin at his woe.

A seal slides down a snowy hill,
Trying tricks that give quite a thrill.
But with one big flop, he flounders away,
Earning laughter on this cold winter’s day.

Frosted whispers bring childlike glee,
Winter's antics, oh so carefree.
In icy jest, we find delight,
As nature plays, beneath the frosty light.

Shards of Winter's Breath

A snowflake lands on a squirrel’s nose,
With a dainty laugh, up it goes.
It sneezes loud, a crisp, clear sound,
As snowflakes spiral gently around.

Chubby snowmen with hats askew,
Wobble about like they've drunk too few.
They try to march, but trip on their feet,
Rolling clumsily, their fate’s bittersweet.

The ice rink buzzes with cheerful blunders,
Where skaters twirl like ships in thunder.
A boy goes down, arms flying wide,
As laughter echoes, it’s quite a ride.

In shards of breath, winter’s tickle plays,
Bringing smiles in wondrous ways.
For in each slip, a tale we weave,
With frosty grins that never leave.

Chasing Crystal Teardrops

Teardrops sparkle from icicle tips,
As children giggle and do funny flips.
They chase the glimmers, darting with glee,
While snowballs fly, oh what jubilee!

A cat in a scarf looks quite absurd,
Dancing in footprints, feeling unheard.
With a sudden bound, it leaps with grace,
And lands in a snowbank, lost in space.

Jolly old snowflakes whisper and spin,
While the world laughs, everyone’s in.
In chase of those droplets, what a delight,
Winter antics bring joy to the night.

With crystal teardrops brightening dreams,
And winter's laughter bursting at seams,
We find the fun in chilly airs,
As chilly gales turn into playful flares.

Embracing the Shimmer

A shiny spike hangs from my eave,
It sparkles bright, it's hard to leave.
I thought it was a candy treat,
But now my tongue is feeling beat.

I put my hat on extra tight,
To catch that glimmer, what a sight!
But with each step I slip and slide,
My dreams of sweet treat now denied.

Each shard of ice a tiny jest,
Just waiting for me to invest.
I reach to grab, I tumble down,
And now I'm wearing frosty crown!

So here I stand, my cheeks aglow,
With winter's prank, I'm feeling slow.
A shimmer laughs as I take flight,
I guess we'll dance through the night!

Dreams Enveloped in Ice

Once I dreamed of a winter ball,
To twirl on ice, I planned it all.
With slippers bright, and style so grand,
But cold hard truth made me quite bland.

I slipped and slid, my spins a mess,
A frosty waltz, I must confess.
I dreamed of grace like swans above,
But landed flat, devoid of love.

A penguin's laugh—I sighed in shame,
As frosty flakes called out my name.
I chiseled dreams of sugar plumes,
But met with icy, frozen dooms.

Now I wear my scarf like a king,
And waddle forth with winter's zing.
With frozen feet, I dance this chance,
In silly steps, I take my stance!

Ethereal Glaciers

Oh, look at those sparkly things up high,
Like frozen dreams in the sky.
I reached for one, a leap, a bound,
But landed flat on icy ground.

Glaciers here, they tease and play,
With shapes that twist in a funny way.
I tried to build a frosty friend,
But all I made was a lopsided end.

They giggle as I dance around,
With winter's cloak—what a silly sound!
A frosty beard, a snowman grin,
I laugh so hard, I can't begin.

So let them shimmer, let them gleam,
These icy visions, a frosty dream.
With every slip, I find delight,
In this winter wonder, pure and bright!

Frosted Echoes of Tomorrow

In a world where frost bites and twirls,
I try to catch those icy swirls.
With each cold step, I dance anew,
But winter's laughter sticks like glue.

I try to build a fortress tall,
But the icy bricks refuse to fall.
They giggle as I shout in vain,
A tower made of frozen grain!

Echoes of laughter fill the air,
As I attempt a frosty flair.
With every slip, my pride does thaw,
A fun-filled winter without a flaw!

Yet here we are, with frosty glee,
Sipping hot cocoa, you and me.
Tomorrow comes with new plans set,
For more funny slips, I won't forget!

Glimmers in a Winter Night

Blinky lights on frosty trees,
A snowman winks, oh what a tease.
With carrot nose and floppy hat,
He tells the world, 'I'm really fat!'

Snowflakes twirl like dancing fools,
While squirrels play their winter rules.
A penguin slips, goes for a ride,
On icy paths, he's full of pride!

Hot cocoa spills in laughter's wake,
The marshmallows pop, oh for goodness' sake!
A snowball fight, we take our aim,
With giggles loud, it's all a game.

As stars twinkle, we jump and cheer,
In this cold land, there's love and beer.
Frosty fun, it warms the heart,
In winter's glow, we'll never part!

Thuja Sighing with Frost

Beneath the branches, whispers play,
A tree complains in a funny way.
“Why do humans love to freeze?
I can’t wear scarves, I’m not a tease!”

Snowflakes laugh as they tumble down,
Covering the ground like a big fluffy crown.
“Hey! Is that a snow dog or just a lump?
Oh wait, it’s human; get ready to jump!”

The garden gnomes now wear a hat,
While squirrels giggle, chitter and chat.
“Let’s throw a party, bring on the cheer!
Frost bites, but laughter’s right here!”

Frosted branches, quite the scene,
With nature jesting, all in between.
So come on out, let’s have a ball,
In frosty fun, we all will fall!

Crystal Dreams in the Shiver

In the chill, a crystal gleams,
It giggles softly, sharing dreams.
"I'd dance on rooftops, oh what a sight!
If only folks would share the light!"

Chubby cheeks all red and round,
As winter's children frolic around.
"Watch me slide on this icy path,
Whoops! I slipped, but let's do the math!"

The frosty air sparkles and giggles,
As everyone trips and does the wiggles.
With cheeks aglow and spirits high,
Laughter erupts like a snowball fly!

So let's embrace this chilly breeze,
With every tumble, we do as we please.
In this wintry wonderland we all strive,
To keep the funny things alive!

Ethereal Shards

Glistening pieces of winter's art,
Float in the air like a fairy's dart.
"Catch me if you can!" they sing with glee,
While children chase them, one-two-three!

Frosty patterns on windowpanes,
Create amusing, chilly frames.
"Oh look, a cat dressed as a ghost!"
It pounces high, but laughs the most.

In a blizzard, the snowflakes laugh,
As they swirl and twist on their whimsical path.
With frosty giggles and playful cheer,
They find joy in every little sphere.

As evening falls, the stars take flight,
In this wonderland of pure delight.
So dare to dream, let laughter blend,
In this chilly magic, joy won't end!

Frost-Edged Fantasies

In the chill of the bright winter sun,
Snowflakes whisper, oh what fun!
A snowman with a silly grin,
His carrot nose is wearing thin.

Frosty windows with a view so neat,
Who knew snowballs could be a treat?
The dog slips, doing a wild dance,
As if he's been caught in a trance.

Chubby cheeks and tongues so bright,
Catch a flake—oh, what a sight!
While penguins slide and take a shot,
At living their best, is that a lot?

With giggles loud, the cold won't bite,
Snowflakes twinkle, what pure delight!
In frosty realms where laughter flows,
Winter's magic is all that glows.

Frosted Serenity at Dawn

The morning blush in pastel hue,
Winter wakes, but what's it to do?
Trees wear coats of glittery lace,
While squirrels dash in a wild race.

Sunshine peeks, with a playful tease,
Chasing shadows among the trees.
A bunny hops with a dapper flair,
Where did it think it had a care?

Birds chirp jokes in high-pitched tones,
As if they're building ice cream cones.
Hot cocoa steam rises, oh so sweet,
In this frosty world, we can't be beat!

Under blankets, cozy and round,
We giggle softly at snowball sound.
Winter's breath, a frosty cheer,
Serenity sparkles, all is clear.

Conversations with the Winter Sky

Above, the clouds play hide and seek,
And snowflakes chat; it’s quite unique!
The sun cracks jokes, a warming ray,
While fluffy friends drift and sway.

Stars peek through the twilight glow,
“Let’s play tag!” they ask below.
The moon chuckles, a silver hue,
“Catch me if you can, just like dew!”

Trees listen in with an overwhelming grin,
Roots so tickled, they begin to spin.
Wind carries whispers of giggling elves,
Creating mischief that no one shelves.

A dance of frost, oh hear the glee,
The winter sky a lively spree!
Laughter lingers in every flake,
A vibrant tapestry we all partake.

Twilight's Glacial Embrace

In twilight's hug, the world turns bright,
Snow sparkles gleefully, a splendid sight.
Kids sled down with giggles and glee,
While dogs in coats dash joyfully.

Mittens lost, oh what a shame,
A snowball fight turns into a game!
Slips and falls with laughter loud,
Here in the winter, we're all so proud.

Frosty breath dances in the air,
With blushy cheeks and tousled hair.
"Who needs heaters?" someone will shout,
When joy in winter's all that's about!

Firelight flickers, the hot cocoa flows,
Tales of snowmen and come what goes.
In winter's magic, we find our place,
With twilight's glacial, warm embrace.

Nuances of a Frigid Mind

In winter's grasp, my thoughts do slide,
Like frosty flakes on a slippery ride.
A brain freeze comes with a silly grin,
Oh, where's my tea? I should have been in!

Noses clash with snowmen, oh what a scene,
They can’t speak back, but they sure can glean.
A brain made of snow, that’s my kind of day,
Just keeping it cool in a funny way!

Chattering teeth with a candy cane smile,
Making snow angels, all the while.
My thoughts drift off like a snowball fight,
In the frosty air, I’m feeling just right!

With skates on my feet, I glide and I trip,
Falling in laughter, oh what a flip!
A jolly good time in the icy expanse,
Lost in the chill, let’s just take a chance!

Echoes of a Frozen Heart

Chilly whispers in the air, oh dear,
A heart encased in frosty cheer.
It thumps like ice with rhythm divine,
Waking the laughter, on a frosty line!

Snowflakes dance like they're on parade,
Every giggle a frosty cascade.
With snow in my hat and ice on my nose,
This frozen heart just giggles and glows!

In a blizzard of joy, I find my way,
Laughter shimmers in the light of day.
Each shiver a chuckle, what a twist,
Melting away worries, no way to resist!

With snowmen grinning, they cheer me on,
Their carrot nose glints like an early dawn.
So raise a glass of frosty delight,
To echo the joy that feels just right!

Dreams Weaving in the Chill

In chilly realms where dreams take flight,
Snowflakes whisper, oh what a sight.
Thoughts knitted with laughter, warm and bright,
Winding through winter's cozy night.

Hours slip by in a laughable haze,
Wrapped up tight in a fluffy maze.
My dreams are frosted like a cake divine,
In this silly world, it’s party time!

The stars above are ice cubes gleaming,
Filling the sky with my wild dreaming.
Each giggle's a snowball, thrown with glee,
In this wonderland, just let it be!

With playful spirits in the freezing air,
Twirling and tumbling without a care.
Life’s snowy shenanigans fill my heart,
In dreams of laughter, we never part!

Surreal Landscapes of Frost

In a landscape blanketed in white,
Penguins tap dance, oh what a sight!
Unicorns prance on an ice-cold slide,
In this surreal world, you can't hide!

Frosty trees wear coats of glittering ice,
Holding the secrets of cold paradise.
Snowball confetti rains from above,
A winter wonderland filled with love!

With penguins sipping cocoa, not a care,
Chill fills the air, but laughter's everywhere.
Frozen flowers bloom in a funny array,
Sprinkling joy in a whimsical play.

So let's frolic in this surreal domain,
Join the snowflakes in a silly refrain!
In frosty laughter, let's roll and glide,
For in this landscape, joy can't hide!

Frosted Whispers

In the fridge, a chill took flight,
A carrot nose, oh what a sight!
He winked at me, with frosty glee,
Said, 'Don’t eat me, just wait and see!'

He wore a scarf made of old strings,
Sipping snowflakes, imagining wings.
A dance in the freezer, what a show,
Laughing with peas in a cold tableau!

Frosted giggles in the air,
With every inch, a frozen dare.
I tossed a snowball, he ducked with flair,
Claiming victory with frosty hair!

The fridge door creaks, a spark of fun,
Where veggies plot, and snowflakes run.
All year long, they dream of this,
Frosted whispers twist in bliss.

Chasing Crystal Shadows

A gleaming snowman chasing light,
Cabbage hat and round eyes bright.
He slipped on ice and did a spin,
Squealed with laughter, a frosty grin!

Crystal shadows dance in glee,
One tripped over, oh dear me!
But up they rose, with arms outspread,
Chasing dreams where no one fled.

A snowball fight on a sunny morn,
With laughter echoing, skies adorned.
But when they fell, all cuddly tight,
A fuzzy pile of pure delight!

In winter's glow, the shadows play,
Sliding along, they've found their way.
Chasing joy beneath the sun,
With every tumble, their hearts have won!

Winter's Silent Lullaby

A snowflake hugged a sleepy tree,
Whispered magic, soft and free.
The branches chuckled, swaying slow,
'What's this dream? Where do we go?'

Pillow fights with puffs of white,
Snowmen snored throughout the night.
Frosty dreams held secrets tight,
As winter sang of stark delight.

The moon peeked in, a silver grin,
While snowflakes danced on roofs akin.
A lullaby spread far and wide,
As snowflakes twirled, the world they'd bide.

Quiet giggles, a frosty hum,
Echoes of fun, where dreams do come.
In winter's arms, we softly sway,
With silly dreams that want to play.

Glimmering Fangs of Frost

Upon the roof, icicles hung tight,
Glimmering fangs, reflecting light.
But one took aim, with no regrets,
'Watch out below!' it quickly frets!

Slipping bravely on the ice,
Frosty critters, oh so nice!
A bumblebee in a winter scarf,
Buzzing joy, it made us laugh.

The sky erupted in a giggly grin,
As snowflakes danced and took a spin.
'Frosty fangs, beware your fate!'
A twig laughed loud, 'You won't escape!'

In this chill, hearts shine bright,
Glimmers of fun in the pale moonlight.
With frosty fangs and spirits high,
We tiptoe past, laughing as we fly!

Ethereal Fragments of Chill

A frosty sneeze can echo wide,
Such chilly joys we can't abide.
With frozen noses we parade,
While snowflakes dance and never fade.

We slip and slide on sheets of white,
The snowman grins, it's quite a sight.
But watch your step, oh heed the call,
For winter's pranks can make you fall.

Hot cocoa flows, a winter treat,
But marshmallows plan their sneak attack fleet.
A taste of chill that's far from bland,
As laughter spreads across the land.

In scarves and mittens, we collide,
A funny tumble down the side.
With giggles bright, our spirits soar,
In fragments frosty, we adore.

Shards of a Frozen Reverie

In dreams of frost, the penguins tread,
With ice cream cones upon their head.
They waddle forth in winter's jest,
While snowflakes giggle, feel their zest.

Snowball fights break out in glee,
With friendly fire we all agree.
A snowy face, all white and round,
Is where the laughter will abound.

The snowmen spray their icy cheer,
With carrot noses, oh so near.
They shrug and dance, a frosty show,
As winter winds begin to blow.

So here we are, in coats so thick,
With humor shared, we find the trick.
In shards of chill, our hearts ignite,
The frozen fun brings pure delight.

Sleepwalking Through the Snow

With sleepy eyes, I roam the night,
Stumbling on each flake of white.
I trip on dreams, oh what a sight,
As winter whispers soft and light.

Snowy blankets pull me down,
The world's a canvas, blue and brown.
But watch me now, I take a dive,
Awake I am, yet half alive!

In pajamas clad, absurd and warm,
I slide and glide in winter's charm.
With laughter floating on the breeze,
I dance with snowflakes, feel at ease.

I wake from dreams of chilly fun,
As morning shines, my race is run.
Yet still I grin, for who could snore,
With snowy glee just at the door?

The Cold Embrace of Night

The moon peers down with icy glow,
A frost-kissed world begins to flow.
In cozy nooks, we sip our tea,
While winter paints its symphony.

The chilly air brings giggles bright,
As snowflakes twirl in wild delight.
With every breath, we puff and blow,
Creating clouds in this frosty show.

As shadows stretch and laughter gleams,
We chase the stars with silly schemes.
A snowman's laugh, so soft and sly,
Takes form beneath the velvet sky.

In winter's grip, our hearts run free,
With chilly hugs and memory.
For in this night, we dance with glee,
In the cold embrace, just you and me.

Shimmering Threads of Winter

Tiny strands of frosty cheer,
Hanging close, they dance and leer.
A chandelier of frozen glee,
Whispering jokes to all they see.

Watch them sway with frosty grace,
In a playful, glimmering race.
Tickling noses, stealing hats,
Giggles echo, how about that?

Luminous strings that tease the sun,
Winking sparkles, oh what fun!
Puppies leap, and children swirl,
In this winter wonder, laughter unfurl!

Frozen jesters, hanging tight,
In the day and in the night.
Mirrors of joy in chilly light,
Creating chuckles, pure delight.

Fractured Reflections in Ice

Broken bits of winter's whim,
In pools where light can almost swim.
Reflections wobble, twist, and bend,
Like silly faces of a friend.

Silly selfies on the ground,
In frozen frames, the laughs resound.
Each crack a joke, each shimmer bright,
Dancing shadows in the night.

Listen close, they spill their tales,
Of penguin slips and fluffy wails.
The silliness, it knows no bounds,
In this realm where laughter sounds.

Snowflake giggles float on high,
As winter whispers, “Oh, my, my!”
Fractured joy in icy streams,
A winter land of funny dreams.

Delicate Crystals on Silken Breath

Glistening gems that softly chime,
Whispering giggles all the time.
Each crystal laughs as it takes flight,
In a world that's chilly but delightfully bright.

Swinging from branches like light-hearted sprites,
They tease the wind with playful bites.
Winking at passersby with glee,
Dancing around like, “Come join me!”

A symphony of sparkles in the air,
Tickling noses with frosty flair.
Winter’s ticklish, oh what a tease,
Laughing along with the playful breeze.

Each breath a shimmer, each sigh a laugh,
Creating snowmen in a funny half.
With a wave and a giggle, off they soar,
In a crystal world of whimsical lore.

Slumbering Visions Beneath the Snow

Underneath the snow, dreams lie still,
Wrapped in fluff, they dream at will.
Yet sometimes, a snicker breaks through,
As frosty creatures peek at you.

Beneath the surface, giggles flow,
As critters share their snowy show.
With chuckles quiet, they plot and scheme,
To wake the world from winter's dream.

What is that? A harmless prank?
A snowball flies from fluffy bank!
Laughter erupts, snow drifts awake,
As winter jokes give a playful shake.

With every flake, a jest, a jest,
In this chilly, cozy nest.
Slumbering visions, secretly bold,
Waiting for laughter to unfold.

Gleaming Stalactites

Up on the roof, they tremble and sway,
Hanging like teeth from a giant, I say.
With a wink and a twist, they melt with a cheer,
Dropping like secrets when you're drawing near.

Snapping and cracking, they dance with delight,
Trying to prank us in the pale moonlight.
But watch your step, they might take the plunge,
An unexpected shower, a frosty lunge!

Helmets are needed, to dodge the cold rain,
A ticker-tape parade, when it's just melt and drain.
With each little droplet, a giggle, a chime,
Nature's own joke, oh what a silly rhyme!

So tiptoe, my friend, and give them a grin,
For these are the treasures that winter lets in.
With laughter and joy, let the fun never cease,
As we celebrate nature's whimsical fleece.

Echoes of a Frozen Fantasy

In the still of night, sounds bounce off the ice,
Things squeak and the creak, quite the playful slice.
Frozen giggles echo, in the crisp, biting air,
Sparkling with mischief, they're quite the rare flare.

What's that? A snowman that's lost its good hat,
A chilly conspiracy from a wandering cat?
Snowballs are flying, like popcorn from trees,
It's winter's own circus; so laugh if you please!

Fortresses made, yet they falter and crack,
Who's behind that pile? Oh wait, it's just Jack!
Rolling in snow, what a sight to behold,
Frozen silliness, oh so daring and bold!

We twirl and we dance, in the glimmering frost,
Under a sky where all caution seems lost.
With joy in our hearts, we embrace the unknown,
In the land of cold whims, we're never alone.

Winter's Lament

Oh, winter can grumble, it frowns with a sigh,
Whispering stories of snacks piled high.
The cocoa is bubbling, with marshmallows bold,
Yet the frostbite's creeping, just watch it unfold.

Puffs of white fluff dance right down with glee,
But watch out for slips! A sight to see!
With sleds that take flight, like creamy soufflés,
We race down the hills, in a blur of white haze.

Let's gather our courage, and rally the crew,
For who needs a plan when the chaos is new?
With laughter a-plenty, we'll welcome the chill,
And turn the cold woes into snowman-filled thrill!

So here's to the season, both frosty and sly,
Where moments are frozen, and time flies high.
In the midst of the fun, oh, we find our own balm,
Winter may grumble, but still, it's so calm.

Glacial Reverie

In a world of blue ice, the sunlight does tease,
A shimmering canvas, as cool as the breeze.
With each gentle crack, it's music's sweet score,
As snowflakes like dancers come waltzing for more.

The chill in the air plays tricks on our heads,
As flurries of giggles tumble out of our beds.
With slippery antics, we shuffle and slide,
Embracing the joy that this coldness can hide.

Laughter erupts, as we ride on the freeze,
Making snow angels with the greatest of ease.
We sculpt out the moments, like art on a spree,
In winter's own gallery, where frolics run free.

So let's toast with icicles (just not on our lips),
To the wonders of winter, with all of its quips.
As sparkles delight, let's forget all our woes,
In this frosty reverie, where joy only grows.

Milton Keynes UK
Ingram Content Group UK Ltd.
UKHW020818141124
451205UK00012B/647

9 789916 945513